Conditioning for Ice Hockey: YEAR ROUND

by PAT CROCE, LPT, ATC
and BRUCE C. COOPER

LP

LEISURE PRESS
New York

A publication of Leisure Press.
597 Fifth Avenue, New York, N.Y. 10017
Copyright 1983 by Pasquale Croce, Jr.
All rights reserved. Printed in the U.S.A.

ISBN 0-88011-090-2
Library of Congress Number 82-83917

Book and Cover design: Brian Groppe
Exercise Photography by: Peter A. Zinner
Typeset by: Bacchus Press, Berkeley, CA

ACKNOWLEDGEMENTS

I wish to acknowlege with thanks the following for their assistance in the preparation of this book: *Bob Clarke* and *Paul Holmgren* of the Philadelphia Flyers who posed for demonstration pictures; the *Philadelphia Flyers management* for providing action photos and continued support; *David Weinstein* of Drexeline Nautilus for facilities for demonstration photos; my secretary, *Lisa Pennacchia*, for typing the final manuscript; and *Bruce Cooper*, whose way with words is second to none.

Pat Croce, LPT, ATC

CONTENTS

PREFACE

No matter what your reasons for playing ice hockey, you can make yourself a better player—and enjoy the game more—by being physically fit. The level of play makes no difference, you play better—and longer—if you adopt a structured, year-round conditioning program.

This book offers a physical conditioning program designed *specifically* for hockey. Whether you are a recreational player or a top professional in the National Hockey League, the program outlined in the following pages will help make you a better hockey player—but *only* if *you* put in the effort required. If you cheat, you will only cheat yourself.

"Winning isn't everything," the old Lombardi adage begins, but we believe that the *effort* to win is! That effort begins the first time a pair of skates is laced to the feet. The *effort* to achieve each goal is the key element required to reach it. *Conditioning For Ice Hockey: Year Round* is a guide to help you efficiently direct your effort to reach your goals as a hockey player.

Ice hockey is unique in its location—on the ice. While many of the physical demands on its players are similar to those in other sports, many others are peculiar to hockey and require special training regimens. The exercises and routines that follow have been scientifically designed not only to meet those special needs of the game, but also to *maintain* those hard earned abilities throughout the playing season. That is the difference between our approach and other more "traditional" ones.

Many hockey coaches and players are under the misconception that conditioning for hockey takes place *only* during the relatively brief period of time between the off-season and the playing season. They think that a few weeks of training camp or pre-season conditioning and practices are all that are required and that games and in-season practices are sufficient to maintain whatever level of conditioning the players may have attained.

Nothing could be further from the truth!

It is now well established that

athletes in most sports in fact tend to become *de*conditioned during the course of the season so that by the time they reach the most important time of the playing year—the play-offs—they are in a far lower state of conditioning than they were on opening day. The philosophy of *Conditioning For Ice Hockey: Year-Round* is to lead to the conditioning peak at play-off time.

Most athletes have preferences on what types of exercises they like to do and often tend to concentrate on those at which they excel while neglecting those they find more difficult. That may make training less arduous, but it *also* makes it far less effective. This program is designed to be followed *as a whole*

in order to provide balanced development of every part of the body. If you fail to follow through in *each* area of training, much of your effort will be wasted.

Unlike many other team sports, hockey requires that you *both* be able to operate efficiently in short spurts of intense work (*an*aerobic exercise) during your on-ice shifts AND develop the capacity to recover quickly and repeatedly during relatively brief rest periods on the bench (aerobic endurance). The most productive players, i.e. the most *physically fit*, are those who are able to perform consistently in the final minutes of the game as they did in the opening shift. When playing against teams of roughly the same age and skill level, the

single factor which most often makes the difference between winning and losing is physical conditioning.

Conditioning is a state of being that requires effort to maintain as well as to achieve. For that reason, you must be willing to devote effort on a year-round basis; that means in the off-season as well as pre-season and in-season. If you fail to follow through, the benefits and results of your previous effort will disappear.

In addition to specific goals for the Off-Season, Pre-Season, and In-Season portions of the calendar year, the overall program is broken down into *four* main areas of conditioning—*Flexibility, Muscular Strength, Muscular Endurance* and

Cardiovascular Endurance. Each of these four areas is important for different reasons which will be explained more fully throughout the book. It is impossible to over-state the importance of attaining a high level of devlopment in *all* four of them. They are irreconcilably interrelated.

There is one further benefit of following a year-round program of conditioning for hockey which we have not yet mentioned. *Injury prevention.* Its importance should not be underestimated. As conditioning improves, players will be less prone to injury, especially the strains, muscle pulls and aches and pains associated with intense, high-speed contact sports such as hockey. *Conditioning for Ice Hockey: Year Round* should not only lead to better performance on the ice but also help *keep* you on the ice.

The objective of the program is physical conditioning that will help you become a better hockey player by improving your strength, endurance and quickness while also making you less susceptible to injury.

Now it is up to *you* to put in the effort required to make yourself a winner on the ice as well as off.

"SEASONAL" CONDITIONING

1

*I*ce hockey, as with most sports, is a "seasonal" game. But conditioning for hockey requires year-round effort. For training purposes, we have divided the year into three parts—*Off-Season, Pre-Season,* and *In-Season.* The specific conditioning goals of each is different but one ingredient of work is common to all three—*intensity.*

In order for a year-round conditioning program to be of benefit, it must be followed religiously regardless of the season. Effort will produce results. But slacking off will not only lead to *no* improvement, but will lead to *deterioration.* It is not enough to achieve physical fitness. You must also work to *maintain* it.

While the particular aims of the three conditioning "seasons" are different, together they are designed to provide a balanced program to develop the body to function at greatest efficiency. And the more efficiently it is possible to work, the less fatigue will develop and the greater will be the reserve late in the game when it is needed most.

Off-Season conditioning concentrates on building a solid foundation of strength, bulk, flexibility and endurance. This is accomplished through *alternating* sessions of short-duration, high resistance training to build bulk and strength AND concentrated aerobic training to improve endurance—the ability of the muscles and cardiovascular system to recover quickly. Flexibil-

ity is worked on daily as it is in the other two seasons.

Pre-Season training starts about six weeks prior to the first organized practice of the year. During this period the pace of training is accelerated and emphasis is shifted from development of strength to endurance. Workouts take the form of *Circuit Training* during which the resistance to be overcome is lowered while the number of repetitions is increased. Endurance is built by shortening the time permitted to complete each exercise in the circuit while simultaneously decreasing the length of rest periods between drills. Pre-Season training, not by chance, is designed to resemble the conditions of the game by requiring short periods of intense, uninterrupted work interspersed with brief periods of rest.

In-Season training is designed to prevent "*de*conditioning" during the playing season. It is well established that the "routine" of hockey season—frequent travel, disruptions in sleeping and practice schedules, and countless other distractions and stresses as well as its length—all work against the maintenance of conditioning. Under these circumstances, the exercise of games and practices is *insufficient* to preserve built up strength and endurance without continued training.

The key element in success or failure with a conditioning program is following it year-round. There is no "vacation" from fitness. If you don't *use* it, you *lose* it!

SEASONAL CONDITIONING

	OFF-SEASON	PRE-SEASON	IN-SEASON
FLEXIBILITY:			
Solo stretch	X	X	X
Partner stretch	X	X	X
Locker stretch			X
Wet stretch		*X	X
MUSCULAR STRENGTH:			
Strength training	X		
MUSCULAR ENDURANCE:			
Dry circuit training		X	X
Wet circuit training		*X	X
CARDIOVASCULAR ENDURANCE:			
Continuous training	X	X	
Interval training		X	X

*If ice time is available

"AEROBIC...
OR *ANAEROBIC?*"

2

"Aerobic...or *an*aerobic? That is the question."

With apologies to the Bard, that is a question to be asked each time you work out. The terms literally mean "with air" and "without air," and are used to describe the two principal ways in which muscles work. It is important to know and understand the difference between the two processes—and why it is important to maximize the capacity of *both.*

Aerobic metabolism is the process by which the muscles receive fuel and oxygen and are cleansed of the byproducts of work, lactic acid and carbon dioxide. This is accomplished by the blood which is delivered to the muscles by the cardiovascular system. Increasing the efficiency of your aerobic metabolism improves your ENDURANCE—the ability to work at a high level of intensity over a relatively long period of time before reaching the point of fatigue, and then being able to recover quickly with rest.

Anaerobic metabolism is the process by which muscles are able to convert *stored* fuel and oxygen into work at a rate *faster* than the blood would otherwise be able to supply and cleanse them. Developing a high level of *an*aerobic fitness is essential to being able to perform at very high levels of intensity over short periods of time without becoming fatigued. This is especially important to a hockey player because he repeatedly must go 'all out' for a minute or two during his on-ice shifts (*an*aerobic exercise) and then recover quickly during brief rest periods on the bench (aerobic capacity).

Virtually *all* of the exercises and regimens in this book are designed to improve one or the other of these capacities. During each exercise, consider how and why it is helping improve fitness in each area. That will help you understand *why* you are being asked to do each exercise and appreciate the importance of balanced development.

Your question to yourself before doing each exercise should always be: "Aerobic...or *an*aerobic? Which it is, and why?"

FLEXIBILITY:
HOW TO STRETCH YOUR CAREER 3

Nothing shortens a hockey player's career faster than injuries, so a key element to any conditioning program for hockey is injury prevention. The best way to avoid the most common and in many ways most debilitating injuries suffered by hockey players—muscle and ligament pulls and tears—is through flexibility training.

Stretching is the *easiest* and most effective way to "stretch" your hockey career. And it only takes a few minutes a day.

You have long been familiar with the importance of warming up before engaging in strenuous physical activity. That is literally what stretching does for your muscles. It raises the temperature *within* the muscles, making them less stiff and more elastic. (Think of a muscle as a stick of chewing gum. If you try to bend a piece that is very cold, it is stiff and will break. But when it is warm, it stretches and bends with ease.)

The effect of stretching and warming the muscles is to increase their maximum length and improve the range of motion of the joints. This not only helps prevent injuries but also enhances dexterity and the ability to exert full power throughout that extended range of motion.

And that, not surprisingly, is the definition of "*power*" in athletics.

Increased power makes a more efficient hockey player. Because you are flexible, you will be able to skate harder and accelerate faster while expending *less* overall energy than a less flexible player because you will not be doing extra work to overcome stiffness and inelasticity in your muscles and joints.

When working on flexibility, you should pay particular attention to developing maximum suppleness and extension in the hips, groin and lower back. A hockey player experiences more stress and strain in these areas than virtually any other parts of the body. Hockey often requires players to be reaching for the puck or shooting while skating in a bent, unnatural position for which the body was not particularly well designed. When you add this to the speed and heavy contact of the game, you have a recipe for injury which good flexibility can help prevent.

In order to be effective, flexibility training must be done *every day* and done properly. The correct way to do any stretching exercise is to do it *slowly* and *smoothly* to the point of maximum extension and then *hold* that position (static stretching) for *at least* ten seconds.

Stretching which is not done properly (slowly, smoothly and held) not only will not result in any improvement, it can also itself cause injury by not allowing tissues to adjust to the stretched position, thereby causing minute breakdowns and tears to occur within the muscle fibers and ligaments.

In order to achieve maximum stretching when working joints with opposing muscle groups, apply full force with whichever muscles are contracted. This will automatically cause the opposing muscle(s) to relax (reciprocal inhibition) and allow it to be fully stretched.

Don't underestimate the importance of stretching *every day*. It takes only a few minutes but those few minutes could make the difference between a relatively injury-free playing career and spending much time on the sidelines.

And for a hockey player, there is no worse feeling than being a spectator, watching your teammates have all the fun.

STRETCHING RULES:
- Perform each stretching exercise in sequence.
- Move your body or segment through its maximum range-of-motion very slowly.
- Maintain the stretched position for at least ten seconds.
- Relax and repeat the exercise again, attempting to go a little further.
- Absolutely no bouncing!
- Concentrate on smooth, regular breathing throughout the stretch.
- Stretch daily.
- Record your stretching routine in the enclosed conditioning diary.

THE SOLO STRETCH

The *Solo Stretch* can be done anytime, anywhere. As it requires no equipment other than yourself, you will probably find that you use the Solo Stretch more often than any of the other three. The rules are simple and very little time is required. As in any stretching exercise, the most important thing to remember is to do it *slowly* and *smoothly*, and to *hold* each position at maximum extension for at least *ten seconds*.

S1. LOW BACK
(ERECTER SPINAE)

Slowly roll backwards with your feet and legs over your head. Keep your hands on your hips for support and attempt to touch your toes to the ground.

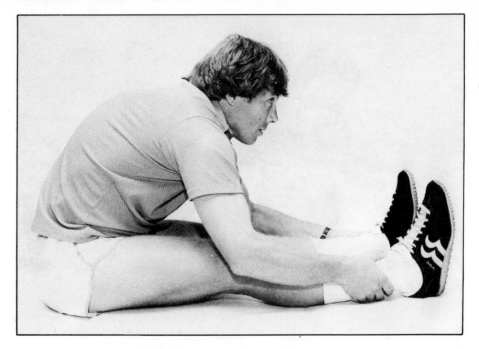

S2. BACK THIGHS (HAMSTRINGS)

Keeping your legs straight and using your hands for assistance, slowly pull your nose to your toes.

S3.   TRUNK TWISTERS
(OBLIQUES)

Slowly push your elbow against your opposite bent knee. Rotate your trunk as far as possible using your hand for support. Repeat to opposite side.

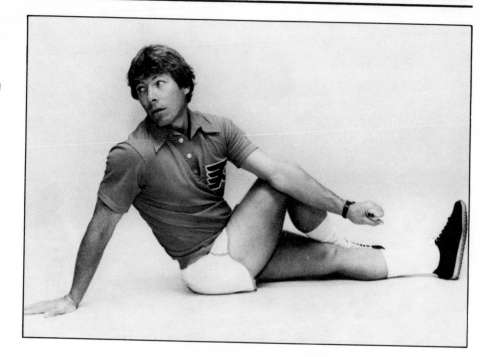

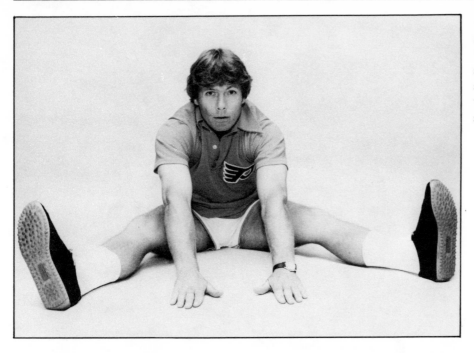

S4. Groin
(ADDUCTORS)
Keeping your legs straight and spread apart as far as possible, slowly lean your extended trunk forward, using your hands for support.

S5. HIP FLEXORS (ILIOPSOAS)

Keeping your front knee directly over your ankle and your back leg straight, slowly lower your hips to the ground. Maintain an erect-back position with your hands on your front knee for support. Repeat with opposite leg.

S6. SHOULDERS
(BICEPS, LATS)
Keeping your arms straight and your fingers interlaced, slowly raise your arms up, over and behind your head with your palms facing the sky.

S7. ARMS
(TRICEPS)

With your arms overhead, reach down your back with one hand as far as possible. Grasp the bent elbow with your other hand and slowly pull it behind your head. Repeat with opposite arm.

S8.　FRONT THIGHS (QUADRICEPS)

With your knee bent and your foot behind your back, grasp the foot with your opposite hand and slowly pull the heel in toward your buttocks. Use your other hand for support. Repeat with the opposite leg.

S9.   CALVES
(GASTROCS)
Keeping your legs straight and
your heels on the floor, slowly lean
your body forward, using your
hands for support.

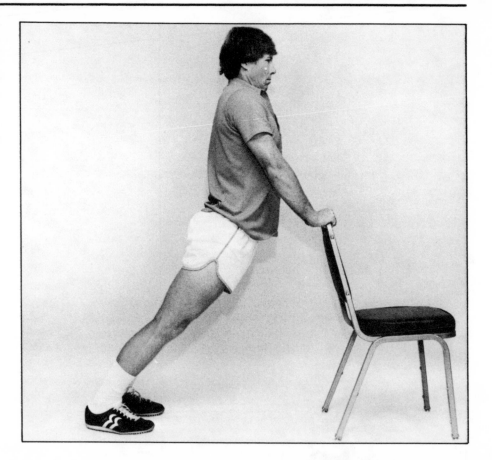

S10. CALVES
(SOLEUS)
Maintaining your heels on the floor with your knees slightly bent, slowly lean your body forward, using your hands for support.

THE PARTNER STRETCH
As the name implies, the *Partner Stretch* requires a second person. The function of the partner is to help you increase the maximum degree of flexion you are able to reach by providing tension. This is done by your partner applying resistance for you to work against at the flexed position and then stretching you even farther when you relax. After completing your stretching exercises, reverse roles and help your partner do the same.

P1. LOW BACK
(ERECTER SPINAE)

While your feet and legs are over your head, your partner grasps the back of your legs slightly above the knees. Attempt to push your legs forward to the ground while your partner resists any movement for six seconds. After the six seconds, relax, and let your partner slowly push you farther back into the stretched position. Hold the new stretched position for ten seconds.

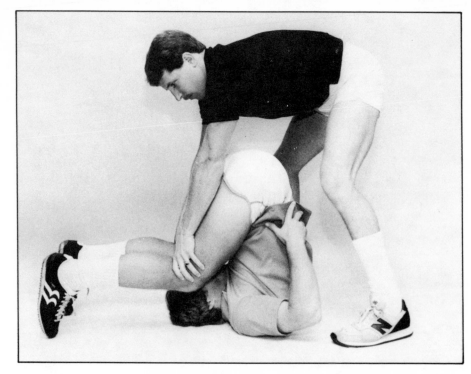

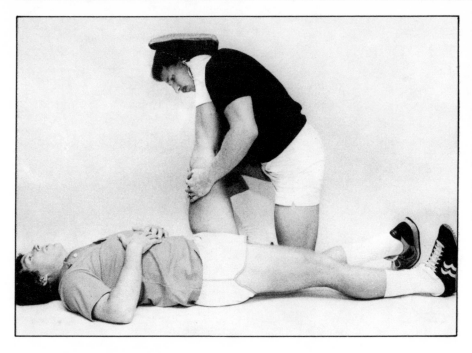

P2.   BACK THIGHS (HAMSTRINGS)

While your leg is *straight* and as high off the ground as possible, your partner grasps it slightly above the knee with your ankle resting on his shoulder. Attempt to pull your heel straight down to the ground while your partner resists for six seconds. Relax, and let your partner slowly push your straight leg farther up into the stretched position. Repeat with opposite leg.

P3.   HIP FLEXORS
(ILIOPSOAS)

Bend your knee; your partner sits on your buttocks (not your back) and lifts the bent leg as high as possible. Attempt to pull your knee down to the ground while your partner resists for six seconds. Relax, and let your partner slowly pull your bent leg farther up and into the stretched position. Repeat with opposite leg.

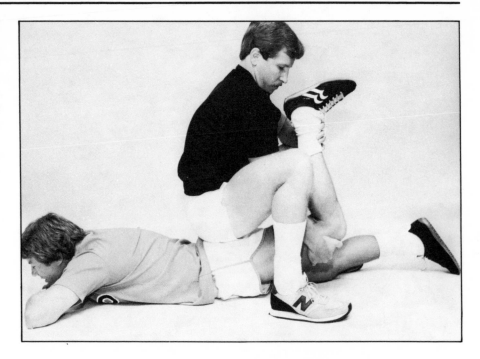

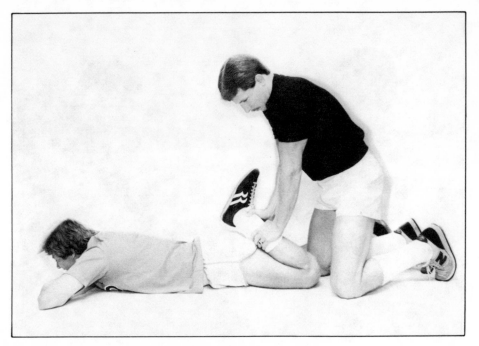

P4. FRONT THIGHS (QUADRICEPS)

Bend your knee as far as possible; your partner grasps your ankle with both hands. Attempt to push your leg straight while your partner resists for six seconds. Relax, and let your partner slowly and carefully push your heels to your buttocks. Repeat with opposite leg.

P5. GROIN
(ADDUCTORS)

While you sit with your legs *straight* and spread apart as far as possible, your partner grasps your ankles. Attempt to pull your legs in together while your partner resists for six seconds. Relax, and let your partner slowly push your legs farther out into the stretched position.

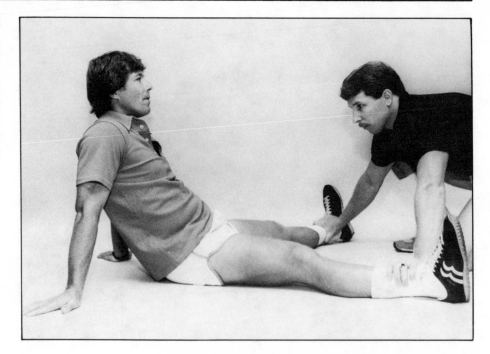

P6. CHEST
(PECTORALS)

As you bend your arms slightly, keeping them at shoulder height, your partner grasps your wrists, making sure to keep your palms up. Attempt to pull your arms in together while your partner resists for six seconds. Relax, and let your partner slowly pull your arms farther back into the stretched position.

P7. TRUNK
(LATS)

While your arms are *straight* and over your head as far back as possible, your partner grabs around your arms with his hands resting on your shoulder blades (your hands are in the air behind your partner). Attempt to pull your straight arms down to your toes while your partner resists for six seconds. Relax, and let your partner slowly pull your arms farther back into the stretched position.

THE LOCKER STRETCH

The *Locker Stretch* is done at your locker stall just before you go on the ice. It requires no more than ten minute's time and helps get you loose for the game or practice, as well as starting to warm up your muscles before you step on the ice. The Philadelphia Flyers of the National Hockey League do the locker stretch religiously before every game or practice.

L1. SHOULDERS
(BICEPS, LATS)

Keeping your arms straight and
your fingers interlaced, slowly raise
your arms up, over, and behind
your head with your palms facing
the sky.

L2. ARMS
(TRICEPS)

With your arms overhead, reach down your back with one hand as far as possible. Grasp the bent elbow with your other hand and slowly pull your elbow behind your head. Repeat with opposite arm.

L3. UPPER BACK
(RHOMBOIDS)

Grasping your opposite elbow, slowly pull your elbow across your chest toward the opposite shoulder. Repeat with opposite arms.

L4. CHEST *(PECTORALS)*

With your arms at shoulder level and your palms up, slowly pull your arms backward, attempting to touch your shoulder blades together.

L5.   TRUNK TWISTERS
(OBLIQUES)

Sitting with one leg crossed over
the other, slowly push your elbow
against your opposite bent knee.
Rotate your trunk as far as possible, using your back hand for support. Repeat to opposite side.

L6. LOW BACK
(ERECTER SPINAE)

With your legs spread shoulder-width apart, grasp your opposite elbow and slowly bend forward as far as possible.

L7.   BACK THIGHS
(HAMSTRINGS)

Keeping your legs straight and
using your hands for assistance,
slowly pull your nose to your toes.

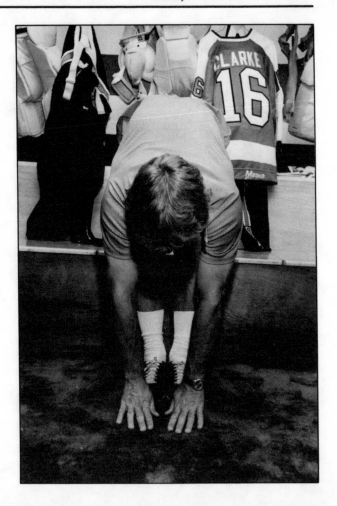

L8.   GROIN (ADDUCTORS)

Keeping your legs straight and spread apart as far as possible, slowly lean your extended trunk forward using your hands for support.

L9. FRONT THIGHS
(QUADRICEPS)

Leaning on your locker with your
knee bent and your foot behind
your back, grasp your foot with
your opposite hand and slowly pull
your heel in toward your buttocks.
Repeat with opposite leg.

L10. CALVES
(GASTROCS)
Keeping your legs straight and your heels on the floor, slowly lean your body forward, using your hands on your locker for support.

THE WET STRETCH

The *Wet Stretch* is designed to be done on the ice. It is not absolutely necessary to do a wet stretch every time you skate *unless* your have not had time to do a locker stretch before stepping on the ice. There is frequently not much space in locker rooms of smaller rinks to do stretching so this is another time when the wet stretch is useful.

W1.   SHOULDERS
(BICEPS, LATS)

Holding your stick with hands shoulder-width apart, keep your arms straight and slowly raise your stick up, over, and behind your head.

W2.   RIB CAGE *(INTERCOSTALS)*

With your stick held overhead, slowly lean to one side as far as possible. Repeat to opposite side.

W3.   TRUNK TWISTERS (OBLIQUES)

Resting your stick on your shoulders behind your head, slowly rotate your trunk to one side as far as possible. Repeat to opposite side.

W4. BACK THIGHS (HAMSTRINGS)

Keeping your legs straight and holding stick with hands shoulder width apart, slowly bend forward touching your stick to the ice.

W5. GROIN (ADDUCTORS)

Keeping your legs straight and spread apart as far as possible, slowly lean your extended trunk forward, using your hands for support.

W6. GROIN
(ADDUCTORS)

Kneel and slowly spread your knees apart as far as possible. Use your hands on the ice for support.

W7. HIP FLEXORS (ILIOPSOAS)

Maintaining one knee on the ice and your other knee bent directly over your ankle, slowly lower your hips to the ice. Keep your back perfectly straight with your hands on your front knee for support. Repeat with other leg.

W8. HIPS & BUTTOCKS *(GLUTEALS)*

Keeping your shoulders on the ice, bend your knee up and over to the opposite side. Grasp your bent knee and slowly pull to the ice. Repeat with other leg.

W9. LOW BACK (ERECTER SPINAE)

Slowly roll backwards with your feet and legs over your head. Keep your hands on your hips for support and attempt to touch your skates to the ice.

MUSCULAR STRENGTH: BUILDING THE "ENGINE"

4

Muscular strength is an important factor in athletic performance and that is especially true for contact sports such as ice hockey. The muscles are an athlete's "engine" and the stronger they are, the better the foundation on which to build all his other performance skills.

While strength training is performed year-round, the off-season is the time to concentrate on building up muscles. To develop them efficiently requires work and dedication, but the most important element is *intensity*. The *only* way to increase strength is by working each set of opposing muscles to absolute fatigue—and then just a little bit more. It is that *extra* little bit of work that provides *100 percent* of the improvement.

Working your muscles beyond their point of fatigue is called the *Overload Principle*. What literally happens is that the muscle tissue breaks down when it is exercised to failure. It is that very breakdown that stimulates it to rebuild itself to a level of greater strength and bulk than before. It is this process, repeated over and over, that builds athletic strength.

Strength is developed by using resistance training in which the resistance the muscles must overcome is increased to the point of muscle failure. If it is not progressively increased with each workout, strength will reach a plateau beyond which no improvement will be noted until resistance is again increased.

As with flexibility training, strength training also helps to prevent injuries through better support of the joints and improved shock absorption due to increased muscle girth. It also helps in the development of "power" (intense work at high speed), an ability which is perhaps more important in ice hockey than in any other team sport.

As mentioned earlier, the upper legs, groin and lower back are a hockey player's physical linchpin. For this reason, particular emphasis should be put on strengthening the muscles of these areas. It is these muscles that are called upon to work hardest in order for you to skate as well as throw body checks and reach for the puck while bent over.

Because strength training involves the breakdown and rebuilding of tissue, it should *never* be done on *consecutive* days or less than 48 hours before a game. If such an interim is not allowed between training periods, the benefit of the original exercise will be *lost*.

While strength training is intense work, it requires only about three hours of actual training time per week to be effective. All that is needed is some type of equipment that provides variable resistance. Free weights, a Universal Gym or Nautilus machines all fit those requirements.

One further guideline that should be observed is to alternate exercises that work the upper and lower halves of the body. This will stimulate circulation. Your workouts should also be designed to progress from the larger to the smaller muscle groups to help prevent undue fatigue.

EXERCISES FOR STRENGTH TRAINING

MUSCLES	FREE WEIGHTS	UNIVERSAL GYM	NAUTILUS MACHINES
1. Chest (pectorals)	Bench press	Bench press station	Double chest
2. Buttocks (gluteals) Thighs (quadriceps)	Quarter squats	Leg press station	Duo squat
3. Back (lats)	Pullovers	Lat pulldowns	Super pullover
4. Thighs (quadriceps)	Knee extensions	Leg extensions	Leg extension
5. Shoulders (deltoids)	Lateral raises	Shoulder press station	Double shoulder
6. Back thighs (hamstrings)	Knee flexions	Leg curl station	Leg curl
7. Back arms (triceps)	Tricep dips	Tricep curls	Triceps
8. Groin (adductors)	Ball squeezes	Leg crossovers	Adductor
9. Arms (biceps)	Arm Curls	Bicep curl station	Biceps
10. Stomach (abdominals)	Sit-ups	Incline sit-ups	Abdominal
11. Forearm/wrist	Wrist curls	Wrist station	Multi exercise (wrist curl)

STRENGTH TRAINING RULES:

- Perform each strength exercise slowly and smoothly.
- Concentrate on proper form...no cheating!
- Avoid twisting or shifting your weight while lifting.
- Breathe properly during lifting by taking a deep breath prior to lifting and exhaling through the mouth during the contraction.
- Perform three sets of ten repetitions of each exercise.
  - a. 1st set (easy): 50 percent of 10 RM.*
  - b. 2nd set (medium): 75 percent of 10 RM.
  - c. 3rd set (hard): 100 percent of 10 RM.

For example: If you can bench press 200 pounds 10 times and no more, than 200 pounds is your 10 RM for the bench press exercise.
  1st set: 50% (200) = 100 pounds.
  2nd set: 75% (200) = 150 pounds.
  3rd set: 100% (200) = 200 pounds.
- When you have completed the third set of an exercise for the full 10 repetitions, increase the 10 RM of that specific exercise by 5 pounds on the following strength training day.
For example: If you completed the 3rd set of bench press at 200 pounds, the next bench press workout would consist

of the following three sets...
  1st set: 50% (205) = 102 pounds.
  2nd set: 75% (205) = 154 pounds.
  3rd set: 100% (205) = 205 pounds.
- Take at least a 30 to 60-second rest between sets.
- Strength train on alternate days.
- Be sure to have a spotter when lifting your 3rd set.
- Record your strength progress in the enclosed conditioning diary.
*10RM is an abbreviation for 10 repetition maximum, which denotes the maximum weight you can lift 10 times.

N1. DOUBLE CHEST

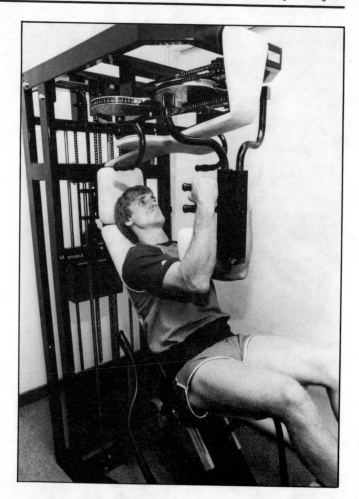

F1. BENCH PRESS
Grasping the bar with your hands approximately double shoulder-width apart, slowly lower the bar to your chest and then push the bar up to a straight arm position. Keep your feet flat on the floor and your buttocks on the bench.

N2. DUO SQUAT

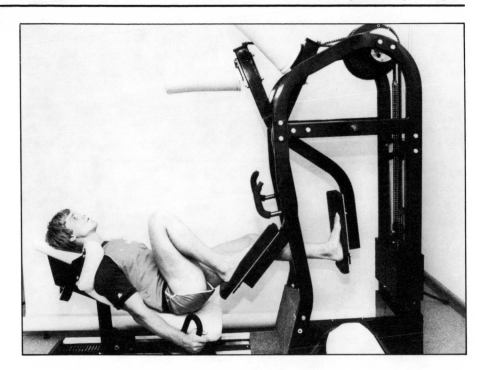

F2. QUARTER SQUATS

With the bar resting on your shoulders behind your neck, slowly lower yourself down to a sitting position on a *high* stool and then stand up. Your feet should be shoulder-width apart and your heels resting on a 2″ high board.

N3. SUPER PULLOVER

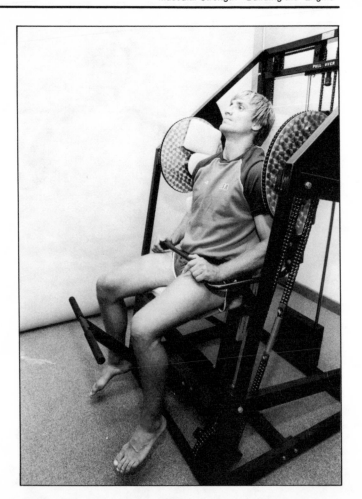

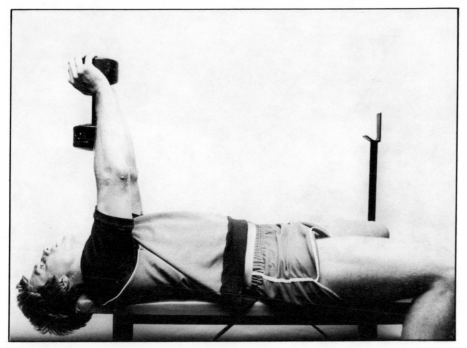

F3. PULLOVERS

Grasping a dumbbell horizontally over your head, slowly raise your arms to a verticle position above your face. Keep your elbows slightly bent during this exercise.

N4. LEG EXTENSION

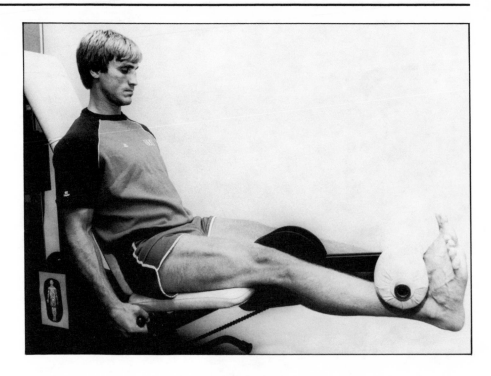

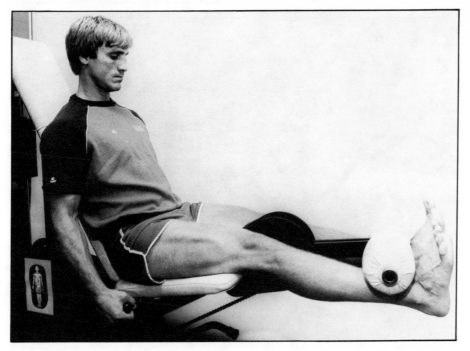

F4. KNEE EXTENSIONS

Keeping your buttocks flat on the seat, slowly kick your legs up to the straight leg position.

N5. DOUBLE SHOULDER

F5. LATERAL RAISES
With a dumbbell in each hand, slowly raise the weights sidewards and up to shoulder height. Keep your elbows slightly bent during this exercise.

N6. LEG CURL

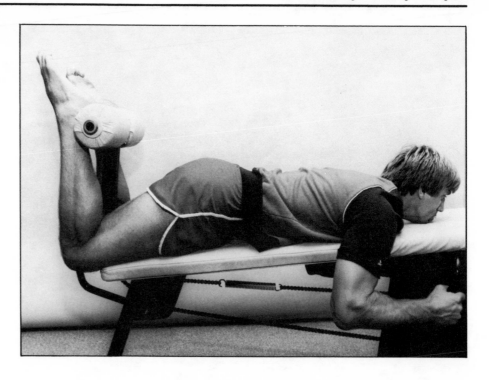

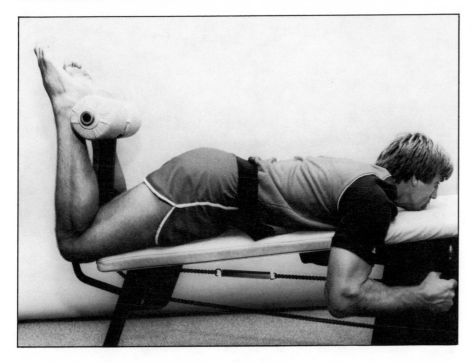

F6. KNEE FLEXIONS

Keeping your pelvis flat on the seat, slowly bend your knees, pulling your heels to your buttocks.

N7. TRICEPS

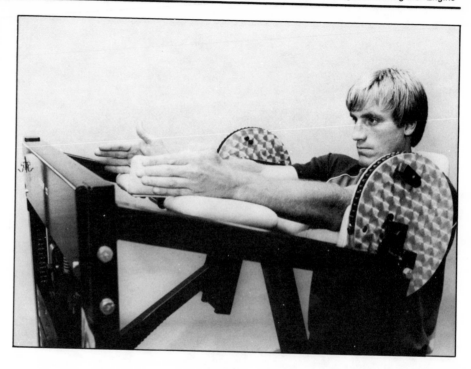

F7. TRICEP DIPS

Leaning backward on a bench with your feet up on a chair, slowly dip down until your elbows are at a right angle and then push up to a straight arm position. Your training weights rest on your lap.

N8. ADDUCTOR

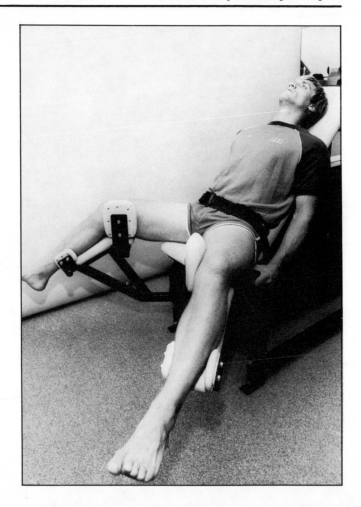

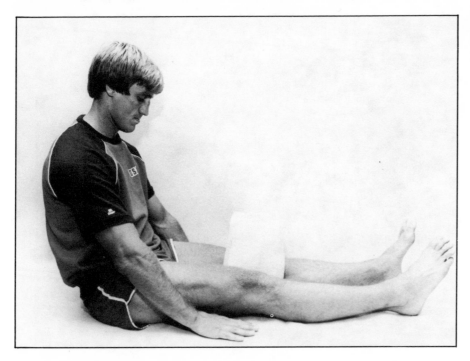

F8. BALL SQUEEZES
With a rubber ball or towel roll resting between your *straight* legs, slowly squeeze your legs together.

N9. BICEPS

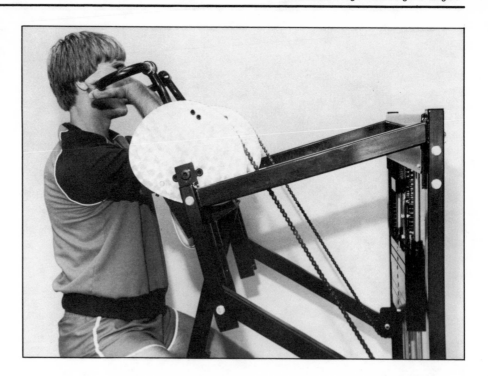

F9. ARM CURLS

Grasping the bar with your hands shoulder-width apart, slowly bend your elbows pulling the bar to your chest. Keep your back flat against the wall by placing your feet approximately one foot from the wall, shoulder-width apart, and your knees slightly bent.

N10. ABDOMINAL

F10. SIT UPS

Lying with your knees bent, feet flat on the floor, and your hands clasped behind your head, slowly sit up and touch your elbows to your knees. Your training weights are held behind your head.

N11. MULTI EXERCISE
(Wrist curl)

F11. WRIST CURLS
Resting your elbows on your thighs with your wrists hanging over your knees, slowly pull your wrists up. Perform this exercise with your palms up and then with your palms facing down.

MUSCULAR ENDURANCE

5

Muscular endurance is the capacity to maintain strength, virtually undiminished, over an extended period of strenuous exercise. A player whose endurance is poor will become increasingly ineffective as the game progresses. A well-conditioned player, however, will be able to contribute as much to helping the team win in the final shift of the night as in the first.

Hockey is basically a game of *control*. The team that is able to maintain control of the puck for more of the playing time than the other most often wins the game. And the key to maintaining control in a heavy contact sport such as hockey is strength. Therefore, all other things being equal, the team whose players have attained the higher level of muscular endurance has a built-in advantage.

The most effective way to develop muscular endurance is through *Circuit Training*—a series of relatively high intensity exercise drills performed sequentially with little or no rest between exercise stations. This builds endurance by requiring the body to do concentrated work for short periods of time (30 to 60 seconds) without providing the cardiovascular system (heart and lungs) enough time during the brief rest periods to fully remove the waste byproducts from the muscles and resupply them with fuel and oxygen.

Wastes, in the form of lactic acid and carbon dioxide (CO_2), act as a "poison" to muscle tissue. Until the cardiovascular system has time to remove them, they both cause pain (soreness) and occupy the space within the muscles needed for the new supply of fuel. When this occurs, muscles lose their ability to contract and performance fades. It is then that the more fit player—and *not* necessarily the more skilled—will most often win the battle for control of the puck.

The beauty of circuit training is that it both *increases* the amount of work that the muscles can do before wastes build up by improving their efficiency AND enables them to *endure* higher levels of lactic acid over longer periods before fatigue sets in and performance diminishes. That is the definition of *anaerobic* fitness. (It should also be noted that circuit training develops *aerobic* fitness as well by requiring high intensity work for at least fifteen minutes per circuit.)

The circuits that follow are designed to be performed on (wet) or off (dry) the ice, with or without weights, and with or without a partner. This provides variety which, experience shows, tends to increase the intensity with which you will be willing to train. It also enables circuit training to be tailored to the available time and equipment.

The main difference between training for muscular endurance and for strength is that circuit training requires greater numbers of repetitions at lower overall resistance and with shorter rest periods.

CIRCUIT TRAINING RULES:
- Perform each exercise as quickly and explosively as possible.
- Concentrate on proper form...no cheating!
- Concentrate on proper breathing, exhaling on effort.
- Continue the exercise until the designated time period is exhausted...no stopping!
- Move from one station to the next immediately.
- As you progress, attempt to increase the number of repetitions and/or the resistance.
- Always attempt to increase speed.
- Record progress in the conditioning diary.

DRY CIRCUIT A
- 11 Stations (same exercises as strength training)
- Alternate each station with some form of high intensity aerobic exercise:
  - Bicycling
  - Rope skipping
  - Running on rebounder
- The weight at each exercise station should be light enough to allow at least 20 repetitions.
- Exercise for 30 seconds. Rest for 15 seconds.
- Total circuit time: 16½ minutes.
- Perform entire circuit *once*.

EXAMPLE: (using free weights)

1. Bench press—30 seconds
   Rest—15 seconds
   Bicycling—30 seconds
   Rest—15 seconds

2. Quarter squats—30 seconds
   Rest—15 seconds
   Bicycling—30 seconds
   Rest—15 seconds

3. Pullovers—30 seconds
   Rest—15 seconds
   Bicycling—30 seconds
   Rest—15 seconds

4. Knee extensions—30 seconds
   Rest—15 seconds
   Bicycling—30 seconds
   Rest—15 seconds

5. Lateral raises—30 seconds
   Rest-15 seconds
   Bicycling—30 seconds
   Rest—15 seconds

6. Knee flexions—30 seconds
   Rest—15 seconds
   Bicycling—30 seconds
   Rest—15 seconds

7. Tricep dips—30 seconds
   Rest—15 seconds
   Bicycling—30 seconds
   Rest—15 seconds

8. Ball squeezes—30 seconds
   Rest—15 seconds
   Bicycling—30 seconds
   Rest—15 seconds

9. Arm curls—30 seconds
   Rest—15 seconds
   Bicycling—30 seconds
   Rest—15 seconds

10. Sit-ups—30 seconds
    Rest—15 seconds
    Bicycling—30 seconds
    Rest—15 seconds

11. Wrist curls—30 seconds
    Rest—15 seconds
    Bicycling—30 seconds
    Rest—15 seconds

DRY CIRCUIT B

- Six stations
  1. Inclined push-ups
  2. Step ups
  3. Pull-ups
  4. Side steps
  5. Tricep dips
  6. Lateral hops
- Perform 10 "explosive" repetitions at each station.
- Move from one exercise station to the next as fast as possible (no rest).
- Circuit takes approximately 1½ minutes to complete.
- Rest three minutes following circuit.
- Perform entire circuit *five times*.
- Total circuit time: 22½ minutes.

EXERCISE DESCRIPTION:

1. **Inclined push-ups**
   Push-up position with feet up on a chair. Touch your chest, push up, and clap your hands.

2. **Step ups**
   Stand facing a 6″ stool with a 10 or 25 pound weight in your hands; step up with your right foot, followed by your left foot, then down with your right foot, left foot.

3. **Pull ups**
   Hanging from a horizontal bar with your palms away from your face, pull up until your chin clears the bar.

4. **Side steps**
   Standing next to a 6″ stool with your right foot on the stool, jump to the right of the stool simultaneously landing your right foot to the right of the stool and your left foot on the stool. Return to starting position by reversing the jump.

5. **Tricep dips**
   Leaning backwards with your hands on one chair and your feet up on another chair, dip down so that your elbows bend at a right angle, then push up to a straight arm position.

6. **Lateral hops**
   Standing next to a 6″ stool with a 10 or 25 pound weight held tightly against your chest, jump with both feet side-wards over the stool.

EXAMPLE: Dry Circuit "B"*

1. Inclined push-ups—10 reps
2. Step ups—10 reps
3. Pull ups—10 reps
4. Side steps—10 reps
5. Tricep dips—10 reps
6. Lateral hops—10 reps

Rest—3 minutes

*Repeat the circuit five times, with
a 3 minute rest period between
each circuit.

WET CIRCUIT A

- Nine stations
  1. Figure 8's
  2. Sit-ups
  3. Wall seat
  4. Roll overs
  5. Squat skate
  6. Push-ups
  7. Wrist rolls
  8. Tricep dips
  9. Mountain climbers
- Alternate each station with a sprint skate around perimeter of rink.
- Exercise for 45 seconds.
  Skate for 45 seconds.
  Rest for 45 seconds.
- Total circuit time: 20¼ minutes.
- Perform entire circuit *once*.

EXERCISE DESCRIPTION:

1. Figure 8's
With a 2 or 5 pound weight attached to the end of a broken hockey stick, grasp the handle of the stick and draw a 3 foot high figure 8 in the air using your wrists only. Perform in both directions.

2. Sit-ups
Lying on your back with your knees bent and hands clasped behind your head, sit up and touch your elbows to your knees.

3. Wall seat
Leaning your back on the boards, assume a sitting position with your hips and knees both at right angles.

4. Roll-overs
Sitting on the ice, roll your trunk to the right, touch your nose to the ice, and push up and over to the opposite side.

5. Squat skate
From a squat position skate from blue line to blue line.

6. Push-ups
With stick in hands touch chest to ice and push up.

7. Wrist rolls
With a 5 or 10 pound weight hanging from a bar, roll the weight up the bar, then unwind the weight by rolling your wrists in the opposite direction.

8. **Tricep dips**
   Leaning backward on a bench, dip down until your elbows are at a right angle, then push up to a straight arm position.

9. **Mountain climbers**
   Resting on the ice on your hands and skates, simultaneously pull your right knee up to your right elbow and push your left leg backwards. Repeat with opposite leg.

EXAMPLE:

1. Figure 8's—45 seconds
   Skate (clockwise)—45 seconds
   Rest—45 seconds

2. Sit-ups—45 seconds
   Skate (counterclockwise)—45 seconds
   Rest—45 seconds

3. Wall seat—45 seconds
   Skate (clockwise)—45 seconds
   Rest—45 seconds

4. Roll overs—45 seconds
   Skate (counterclockwise)—45 seconds
   Rest—45 seconds

5. Squat skate—45 seconds
   Skate (clockwise)—45 seconds
   Rest—45 seconds

6. Push-ups—45 seconds
   Skate (counterclockwise)—45 seconds
   Rest—45 seconds

7. Wrist rolls—45 seconds
   Skate (clockwise)—45 seconds
   Rest—45 seconds

8. Tricep dips—45 seconds
   Skate (counterclockwise)—45 seconds
   Rest—45 seconds

9. Mountain climbers—45 seconds
   Skate (clockwise)—45 seconds
   Rest—45 seconds

WET CIRCUIT A

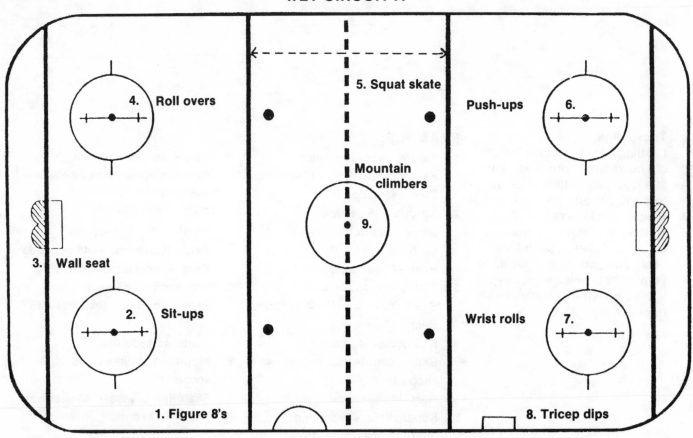

5. Squat skate

4. Roll overs

Push-ups

6.

Mountain
climbers

9.

3. Wall seat

2. Sit-ups

Wrist rolls

7.

1. Figure 8's

8. Tricep dips

WET CIRCUIT B*

- Eleven stations
  1. Sprints (blue line to center line)
  2. Forward circle skate
  3. Push-ups
  4. Apollo skate
  5. Circle keep away
  6. Backward circle skate
  7. Knee drop (goal line to goal line)
  8. Sit-ups
  9. Partner pull (goal line to blue line)
  10. Boards keep away
  11. Tricep dips
- Exercise for 30 seconds. Rest for 15 seconds.
- Total circuit time: 16½ minutes.
- Perform entire circuit *twice*.

*This circuit requires a partner.

EXERCISE DESCRIPTION:

1. **Sprints**
   Sprint from center line to blue line.
2. **Forward circle skate**
   Skate forward around circle.
3. **Push-ups**
   With stick in hands, touch chest to ice and push up.
4. **Apollo skate**
   Attached to the harness of an apollo (pulley-like device), skate across ice pulling your partner in the opposing harness.
5. **Circle keep away**
   Keep the puck away from your partner, using the circle as the boundaries.
6. **Backward circle skate**
   Skate backwards around circle.
7. **Knee drop**
   Start at goal line and skate to opposite goal line, touching your knee at every intersecting line (blue line, center line, blue line).
8. **Sit-ups**
   Lying on ice with knees bent and hands clasped behind head, sit up and touch elbows to knees.
9. **Partner pull**
   With partners facing each other and grasping the same stick, skate backwards, pulling your partner from the goal line to the blue line. Return to the goal line with other partner pulling.

10. Boards keep away
Keep the puck away from your partner using the boards behind the goal and the blue line as your boundaries.

11. Tricep dips
Leaning backward on a chair or bench, dip down until the elbows are at a right angle, then push up to a straight arm position.

EXAMPLE:

1. Sprint—30 seconds
   Rest—15 seconds
2. Forward circle skate—30 seconds
   Rest—15 seconds
3. Push-ups—30 seconds
   Rest—15 seconds
4. Apollo skate—30 seconds
   Rest—15 seconds
5. Circle keep away—30 seconds
   Rest—15 seconds
6. Backward circle skate—30 seconds
   Rest—15 seconds
7. Knee drop—30 seconds
   Rest—15 seconds
8. Sit-ups—30 seconds
   Rest—15 seconds
9. Partner pull—30 seconds
   Rest—15 seconds
10. Boards keep away—30 seconds
    Rest—15 seconds
11. Tricep dips—30 seconds
    Rest—15 seconds

Repeat entire circuit.

WET CIRCUIT B

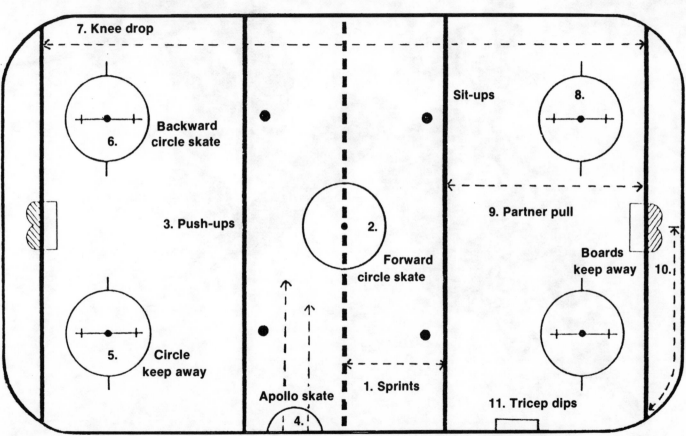

7. Knee drop

6. Backward circle skate

3. Push-ups

5. Circle keep away

Apollo skate

4.

2. Forward circle skate

1. Sprints

Sit-ups

8.

9. Partner pull

Boards keep away

10.

11. Tricep dips

CARDIOVASCULAR
ENDURANCE

*C*ardiovascular endurance—the capacity to *efficiently* cleanse the muscles of wastes and resupply them with fuel and oxygen—is probably more important to hockey players than it is to athletes in any other team sport. Hockey demands its participants work at maximum intensity (*an*aerobic exercise) during on-ice shifts and then recover during brief rest periods on the bench. It is during these rest periods that cardiovascular endurance makes the difference between a quick recovery and no recovery at all.

If you can't breathe, you can't play hockey. It's as simple as that.

Cardiovascular endurance is built through aerobic training. It is a *year-round* process that requires

hard work. But it is hard work that will return even greater rewards. One of the main reasons that the United States Olympic Hockey Team—a diverse group of young and relatively inexperienced American college hockey players—won the Gold Medal at the XIII Winter Olympic Games in 1980 over much higher rated and more experienced teams was their team-wide exceptionally high level of cardiovascular endurance.

The development and maintenance of cardiovascular endurance is a continuous process which must be worked on religiously throughout the playing career. It requires training for at least 15 to 30 minutes per day at a level sufficient to maintain a pulse rate of 60

percent to 85 percent of your maximum (see chart) during the *entire* exercise period. (The above-average athlete should be able to maintain a pulse rate above 70 percent of maximum.)

As a rule of thumb, your maximum heart rate (pulse) as an athlete should be roughly 220 *minus* your age. A 20-year old, well-conditioned athlete, for example, would have a maximum heart rate of approximately 200 beats-per-minute and would therefore need to work hard enough to maintain his pulse between *140* (70 percent of maximum) and *170* (85 percent) beats-per-minute for at least 15 to 30 minutes.

(In order to assure yourself that you are getting the full benefit of your workout, you should check your pulse rate periodically during training. This can be accomplished easily by feeling for your pulse in your neck [carotid artery], counting the beats for ten seconds, and multiplying by six.)

Aerobic training for cardiovascular endurance will enable you to increase the amount of work you can do in a fixed period of time while decreasing the amount of effort needed to do that work. This is the result of increased lung capacity which processes more air with less effort, a stronger heart which can pump a greater volume of blood with *fewer* strokes (decreased heart rate and an increased overall blood volume which has the capacity to carry more oxygen to the muscles. Aerobic training also improves the efficiency of the circulatory system (blood vessels) by increasing its capacity, developing collateral circulation and lowering blood pressure.

Conditioning for ice hockey demands the development of high levels of both aerobic and *anaerobic* fitness. Hockey puts great emphasis on the ability of its players to go all out every time they are on the ice. But if they are unable to recover before their next shift, they will soon become completely fatigued.

There are two principle methods appropriate to achieving cardiovascular fitness—*Continuous Training* and *Interval Training*.

Excellent results—as long as you put in the effort—can be accomplished with either. You can use either or alternate between the two as you please. The only requirement for success is hard work.

EXERCISE HEART RATES

AGE	MAXIMUM HEART RATE	MINIMUM TRAINING RATE (70 percent of M.H.R.)	MAXIMUM TRAINING RATE (85 percent of M.H.R.)
14	206	144	175
16	204	143	173
18	202	141	172
20	200	140	170
22	198	139	168
24	196	137	167
26	194	136	165
28	192	134	163
30	190	133	161
32	188	132	160
32	186	130	158
36	184	129	156

CONTINUOUS TRAINING

Continuous training is as simple as it sounds. Select an activity which provides a continuous demand on the cardiovascular system such as running, skating, swimming or cycling (either stationary or on-the-road) and work at it at a steady pace for a MINIMUM of fifteen minutes. As cardiovascular efficiency improves, lengthen training time and intensity. However, research suggests that the benefits of work tend to diminish for exercise beyond one hour.

As with all exercise, results are achieved *only* through intense work over a period of time. Therefore if you *de*crease the level of intensity of your workout you must *in*crease the length of time you exercise to obtain the same aerobic benefit.

To help avoid the fastest and most common killer of physical fitness programs—boredom—you can add variety to your workout through the technique known as "fartlek training." This simply means that the pace and style of the chosen activity are varied as long as the heart rate does not drop below the aerobic training minimum of 70 percent of maximum at any time during the workout.

If the exercise is skating, for instance, you sprint, skate backwards, side-to-side, crossover, stop-and-start, etc., and at various speeds. If swimming, you can change strokes as well as speeds every lap or so. (The two most beneficial strokes to build fitness for hockey are freestyle, which improves endurance faster than any other, and the breaststroke, which requires extra work for the chest and groin muscles.)

Proper equipment is the key if you choose running or skipping rope. It is important to wear good, well-made running shoes that have a flared heel at least one inch thick in order to provide adequate support for your weight. For jumping rope, select one that reaches just to the bottom of the ribcage when you stand on its center and pull it taut against your sides.

CONTINUOUS TRAINING EXERCISES:

Skating
Running
Bicycling
Swimming
Arm Bicycling
Stair Running
Rope Skipping
Rowing Machine
Cross-Country Skiing Machine

INTERVAL TRAINING

Interval training is similar to continuous "fartlek" training, the difference being in the relative intensity of work performed during the alternating exercise and relief periods. In continuous training, the sustained pulse rate remains fairly stable while in interval training it varies. During "relief" periods it will fall to near the 70 percent minimum needed for cardiovascular endurance training but will more closely approach the absolute maximum during exercise bursts. Done properly, interval training will give roughly the same training effect as continuous training while lessening overall fatigue by providing relief periods during exercise.

Interval training more closely resembles the nature of hockey by simulating the physical demands of on-ice shifts. While on the ice, players are frequently called upon to expend brief bursts of energy at close to maximum cardiovascular capacity interspersed with periods of less strenuous exercise.

As with muscular endurance training, interval training helps improve *an*aerobic fitness during the periods of high intensity exercise while building aerobic capacity by *never* letting the heart rate drop below the 70 percent minimum during relief periods. (This does *not* mean, however, that interval training replaces other *ana*erobic training regimens. It is important to do those, too.)

In order to obtain maximum benefit from interval training (and "earn" the relief periods), it is absolutely essential to go *all out* during each and every maximum intensity interval. Do each as if you were the last man back in the final seconds of a tie game and had to make up three steps on an opposing player in full flight on a breakaway. If you train that way, you *will* catch that man when the situation arises—and it will. It is the physical capacity to make plays like that which separates champions from also-rans. You'll never be a champion if you cheat during training.

If skating is the interval training exercise, use the relief periods to work on skating technique (stride, arm movement, full extension of hips and legs, etc.) as you skate. This will not only help you skate faster but also with less effort (and fatigue) as your skating becomes more efficient with improved technique.

RUNNING INTERVAL PATTERNS
QUARTER RUNNING PATTERN:
1. Run a quarter mile
2. Walk for 30 seconds
3. Run a quarter mile
4. Walk for 30 seconds
5. Repeat this sequence 10 times.

PYRAMID RUNNING PATTERN:
1. Run a quarter mile
2. Walk for 30 seconds
3. Run a half mile
4. Walk for 30 seconds
5. Run a mile
6. Walk for 30 seconds
7. Run a half mile
8. Walk for 30 seconds
9. Run a quarter mile
10. Walk for 30 seconds

STRAIGHTS AND CURVES RUNNING PATTERN:
1. Use a running track or an equivalent city block
2. Sprint the straights
3. Jog the curves

SKATING INTERVAL PATTERNS

Z SKATING PATTERN:

1. Start at goal line
2. Sprint to far blue line
3. Return to near blue line
4. Sprint down to far goal line
5. Coast back to start

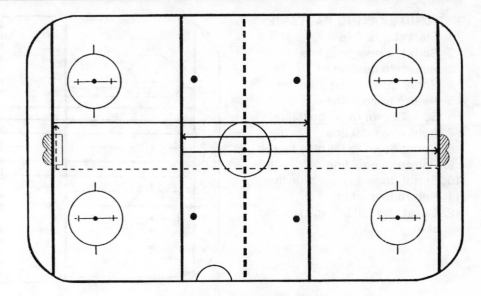

Z SKATING PATTERN

Sprint Distance: 100 yards

_____Sprint
_ _ _ _ _ _ _ _ _ _ _ _ _ _ _ _ _ _ Coast

PYRAMID SKATING PATTERN:
1. Start at goal line
2. Sprint to near blue line
3. Return to goal line
4. Sprint down to far blue line
5. Return to goal line
6. Sprint down to far goal line
7. Return to goal line
8. Sprint down to far blue line
9. Return to goal line
10 Sprint down to near blue line
11. Return to goal line
12. Coast one full lap and back to start.

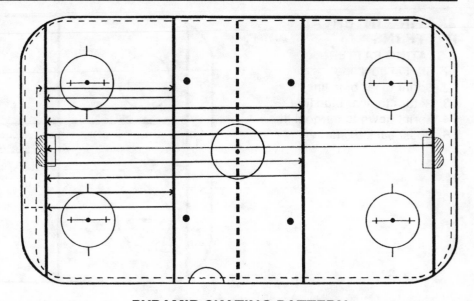

PYRAMID SKATING PATTERN

Sprint Distance: 360 yards

_____Sprint

_ _ _ _ _ _ _ _ _ _ _ _ _ _ _ _ _ Coast

X & O SKATING PATTERN:

1. Start anywhere
2. Skate either a figure 8 or around perimeter of rink
3. Sprint from blue line to blue line
4. Coast the remaining distance
5. Patterns may be interchanged

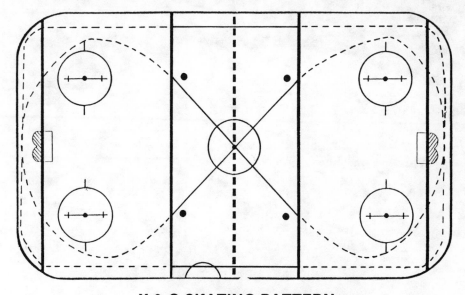

X & O SKATING PATTERN

Sprint Distance: 40 yards

_____ Sprint
- - - - - - - - - - - - - - - - Coast

*T*here is perhaps no area of sports in which ignorance and "faddism" are more prevalent than nutrition. Our purpose is *not* to tell you what and how to eat, but to offer a simple philosophy of nutrition which should help you play hockey more efficiently and with less fatigue. It is a philosophy based on common sense.

Experience shows that no matter how good your physical condition may be, if you do not supply the muscles—and brain—with the fuels needed to function, you won't be able to perform on the ice. The purpose of physical conditioning, in its simplest sense, is the efficient conversion of fuel into work. But if you don't supply your body with that fuel by eating an adequate and balanced diet, that efficiency won't do you much good.

An active, well conditioned hockey player requires about 5,000 calories-per-day but that will vary among individuals depending on such factors as efficiency of metabolism (the chemical process of converting ingested food to usable energy), age, weight, etc. The only difference between the nutritional needs of athletes and other people is that athletes require more calories because they expend more energy. It's as simple as that. As long as the diet is balanced, the body itself will regulate the amount of food intake through increased appetite.

Virtually all foods can be placed in one of four major categories called the *Four Food Groups.* They are:
• *Milk*
• *Meats*
• *Fruits and Vegetables*
• *Breads and Cereals*
Placement of a food into a group is based on the type of proteins, carbohydrates and/or fats which it contains and not necessarily its origin. Peanut butter, beans, legumes, and dried peas, for instance, are all members of the Meat Group because they are rich in the same types of proteins as other members of that group such as red meats, fish, poultry and eggs.

yogurt and ice cream. The Fruits and Vegetables Group consists of green and yellow vegetables, fruits and fruit juices, among other things. Enriched and fortified breads, cereals, rice and pastas are all members of the Breads and Cereals Group. You can achieve balance in your diet by eating *two* servings *each* from the Fruits and Vegetables and Breads and Cereals Groups for a single serving from each of the Milk and Meat Groups.

Carbohydrates, proteins and fats are the substances which the body converts through metabolism to produce the fuels needed by the muscles to contract and for the body to constantly rebuild itself. Vitamins and minerals, on the other hand, most often serve as catalysts which improve the efficiency of metabolism and help maintain the body in health.

Because the digestion of food requires work by the body, *when* you eat is in many ways as important as *what* you eat. If you eat too long—or too soon—before exercise, practice or a game, you will not get the full benefit of your refueling. Here are some guidelines on how to plan your eating to achieve the best results—and help you *win!*

PRE-GAME MEALS:

When and what to eat for a pre-game meal has long been a source of controversy among coaches and athletes. We feel that using common sense is the best approach. The normal emotional tension experienced by athletes as they prepare to enter the competitive arena tends to impede gastrointestinal motility so the pre-game meal should be eaten at least *three* to *four hours* before you step onto the ice. This will allow ample time for digestion and permit the stomach to empty. Exercise on a full stomach will lead to stomach cramps because the blood needed for digestion will be diverted to the muscles of the arms, legs and trunk. That will starve the muscles of the stomach of the fuel and oxygen needed to aid digestion and, like any other muscle, they will react by cramping.

The pre-game meal should consist of foods which are easily digested and readily absorbed. You will want to select a diet which will supply a maximum amount of usable energy delivered at a steady rate over a relatively extended period of time (several hours). As a general guideline, choose foods that are:

• *High* in *Complex Carbohydrates*. Breads, pastas, potatoes, pancakes, skim milk, bananas, cereals, fruits and fruit juices all provide the type of nutrition that is needed in a pre-game meal. Complex carbohydrates supply most of the energy consumed during short, high intensity activity. (As exercise continues, however, fat metabolism plays a more important role in the production of energy.)

• *Low* in *Simple Carbohydrates (Sugars)*. While sugars are the quickest source of energy because they require very little digestion, it is that very property that makes them undesirable. A sudden increase in serum blood sugar triggers the pancreas to produce insulin in order to return the blood sugar to within normal limits. The body tends to overreact in the short term and will actually pull the level down too *low* (rebound hypoglycemia), causing hunger and loss of energy within a few hours after eating—just when you are getting ready to play. Concentrated sugars also tend to cause retention of fluids in the gastrointestinal tract by osmotic effect which can lead to nausea, cramping and dehydration. Both of these reactions will make you less able to sustain the high level work required to play hockey just when you need to be able to function most efficiently.

In order to maintain a high serum blood sugar level you can drink a dilute glucose solution (2 percent or less) periodically during exercise. (Ingestion of dilute glucose solutions does not appear to significantly increase plasma insulin concentration.) You can also eat fruits which are rich in fructose. As a complex carbohydrate, fructose is metabolized in the liver which then delivers it to the system in the form of glucose at a relatively slow and steady rate.

• *Low* in *Protein*. Protein is an essential element in the building and repair of the body's tissues, but it is not a very efficient source of energy for athletics. The ingestion of protein-rich foods before exercise may in fact produce adverse side effects. High levels of protein tend to cause the loss of salt and dehydration through increased urination while providing the body with little available energy.

• *Low* in *Fats*. Foods with a high fat content tend to slow down digestion and trigger the release of the hormone enterogastrone which delays the emptying of the stomach.

• *High* in *Fluids*. Intense exercise causes you to lose body fluid faster than you can replace it. In addition to sweating, you are also releasing significant amounts of fluid every time you exhale. The loss of as little as 2 percent of the body weight starts to impair the ability of the body to regulate its temperature and impairs circulation. As the temperature of the muscles increases beyond their temperature of peak efficiency, they start to lose their ability to contract and fatigue quickly.

It is important not only to prepare for the game by drinking plenty of fluids at the pre-game meal (at least three glasses), but also to replace them during the game. Failure to replace lost fluids can, in the extreme, lead to heat stroke and death. The best guide to the amount of fluid you should take in during exercise is also the simplest—*thirst*.

Fueling the body is a much more complex process than burning gasoline in an internal combustion engine. When you run out of fuel in an automobile, all you need to do is put more gas in the tank and you are ready to go. But the body requires time and energy to convert fuel from the form you ingest it—food—to a form it can use. Fueling your body for work is something you should plan with care. Once the game starts it is too late to do any major "refueling."

GAME TIME:

As indicated earlier, the most

important nutritional considerations during the game are to maintain a relatively high level of serum blood sugar and avoid dehydration. This is accomplished by drinking sufficient fluids to quench thirst and taking in sugars in the form of fructose or dilute glucose solutions. Be careful, however, not to overdo either as they will result in undesirable side effects.

A balanced diet supplies not only the source of energy needed for the body to do work, but also replenishes it with many other substances (vitamins and minerals) which it requires to function. These substances are essential in the regulation of the composition and volume of the body's fluids (homeostasis). In health, the body is able to maintain homeostasis with a remarkable degree of consistency despite wide ranges of dietary intake and metabolic activity. Under most circumstances, eating a balanced diet will provide sufficient amounts of these substances to keep the system in balance.

However, prolonged exercise can cause *depletion* of several key elements which, if not replaced, can lead to electrolyte imbalance. The three which are of most concern to athletes are *sodium* (Na), *potassium* (K) and *magnesium* (Mg). We call them the "sweaty minerals."

• *Sodium* is ingested in the form of salt (NaCl) and is required to maintain adequate blood pressure. It is also important in regulating the amount of fluids the body retains or excretes. Insufficient sodium levels cause the body to retain fluid while excess sodium causes urination and can lead to dehydration. For this reason salt tablets should be avoided during vigorous exercise as they can lead to nausea, cramping, vomiting, heat exhaustion and heat stroke.

Salting of your food to taste should provide you with adequate amounts of sodium. If your body needs more, your tongue will tell you. Sodium is naturally abundant in meats, fish, poultry, grains, nuts, canned and processed foods, and "junk" or "fast" foods.

• *Potassium* is important in regulating your body temperature during exercise and preventing overheating. It is released by the muscles as they heat up, causing the blood vessels to dilate. This increases the flow of blood which carries heat away from the muscles to the skin where it is radiated through the evaporation of sweat. Insufficient potassium prevents this from occuring and can lead to heat exhaustion and heat stroke.

Potassium is found in abundance in all fruits and vegetables and that is why we recommend that you eat fruit following every workout, practice and game.

• *Magnesium* is necessary for efficient muscle contraction and co-ordination. It is also an important catalyst in the regulation of carbohydrate metabolism. Dairy products, nuts and whole grains are all rich in magnesium.

Good nutrition is important to playing winning hockey and no meal is more important to athletes than breakfast. It is the basis on which a well-balanced diet is built.

The digestive system and nutritional state of the body are at their lowest point when you wake up in the morning and require replenishment. Carbohydrates are supplied by fruits, juices, jams, jellies, breads and cereals. A good breakfast will also help prevent the loss of precious muscle weight during your workout when your caloric expenditure is at its highest.

In summary, a well balanced diet drawing on foods from all four food groups should meet all nutritional requirements. We have purposely *not* supplied a specific diet here.

Our aim instead is to show how good nutrition will help you win hockey games as much as developing good physical conditioning does.

You *are* what you eat. If you eat well, you will have a well-nourished body to condition. If you eat junk, that's exactly what your body will be made of.

The choice is up to you!

In order to realize the maximum benefit of your year-round conditioning program, we feel it is important to evaluate progress periodically through fitness screenings. This will not only provide you with proof of your improvement in black and white, but it will also help to tailor your program, placing emphasis on those areas in which you may be deficient.

All players in the Philadelphia Flyers organization are evaluated formally four times during the year—at the start of training camp, at the end of training camp, at mid-season and after the play-offs. These screenings are a relatively simple but very important tool in helping each player improve while telling us—and them—who is working and who isn't.

You can perform your own informal fitness screening by following the program outlined below. If you do not have access to facilities for the relatively expensive stress test (which requires a treadmill and a cardiologist), you can substitute Cooper's 12-minute run for that portion of your evaluation.

BODY COMPOSITION

1. **Weight**
   a) Weigh on a balanced scale wearing shorts and no shoes.

2. **% Body Fat**
   a) Skinfold measurements
   - Triceps: With your arm hanging freely at your side, skinfold is lifted midway between shoulder and tip of elbow.
   - Scapula: Skinfold is lifted just below the shoulder blade.
   - Iliac crest: Skinfold is lifted just above hip (love handle).
   - Abdominal: Skinfold is lifted one inch to right of the navel.

b) % fat = 5.783 plus (0.153 x sum of four skinfolds).

3. **Girth Measurements**
   a) Neck: Relaxed with eyes straight ahead, measure around largest part.
   b) Chest: Expanded, measure around the breast level.
   c) Waist: Relaxed, measure around the level of the navel.
   d) Arms: Flexed with elbow forming right angle, measure around largest part.
   e) Forearms: Flexed with elbow forming right angle, measure around largest part.
   f) Thighs: Relaxed, measure 6 inches above the center of the kneecap.
   g) Calves: Relaxed, measure 6 inches below the center of the kneecap.

CARDIOVASCULAR ENDURANCE:

1. **Maximum stress test**
   a) Use a treadmill or bicycle ergometer under the supervision of a cardiologist; this progressively difficult test measures your consumption of oxygen on milliliters (ml) per kilogram (kg) of your total body weight per minute (min).
   b) Good score: 50 ml/kg/min

2. **12-minute test**
   a) A less timely, inexpensive test developed by Dr. Kenneth Cooper, the 12-minute test can be performed anywhere and by anyone.
   b) Walk, jog, run as far as you can for a total of 12 minutes.
   c) Record the distance covered
   d) Good score: 1½ miles.

FITNESS SCREENING

NAME: _____ DATE: _____

BODY COMPOSITION:
1. Weight _____ lbs.
2. % Fat
   Triceps _____
   Scapula _____
   Iliac crest _____
   Abdominal _____ _____ %
3. Girth measurements
   Neck _____ ''
   Chest _____ ''
   Waist _____ ''
   Arms   L _____ '' R _____ ''
   Forearms   L _____ '' R _____ ''
   Thighs   L _____ '' R _____ ''
   Calves   L _____ '' R _____ ''

CARDIOVASCULAR ENDURANCE:
1. Maximum stress test _____ ml/kg/min

MUSCULAR ENDURANCE:
1. Push ups _____ reps
2. Sit ups _____ reps
3. Step ups _____ reps

MUSCULAR STRENGTH:
1. Maximum bench press _____ lbs
2. Maximum leg extension _____ lbs

FLEXIBILITY:
1. Hamstrings _____ ''
2. Groin _____ ''

POWER:
1. Vertical jump _____ ''

MUSCULAR ENDURANCE:

1. Push-ups (arm endurance)

    a) From the push-up position with your hands at the sides of your chest and your arms fully extended, touch your chest to your partner's hand, and push up to extended arm position.

    b) Your partner lies on his stomach next to you with his hand flat on the floor under your chest.

    c) Record the number of completed push-ups in one minute.

    d) Good score: 45 repetitions.

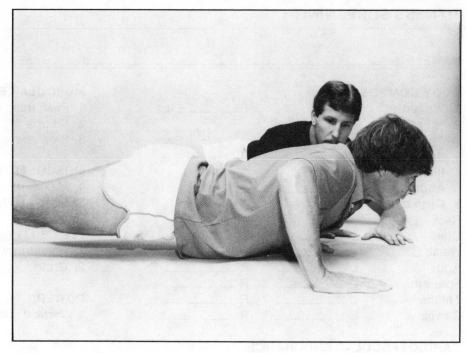

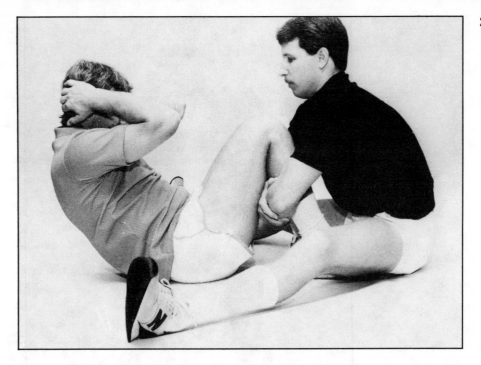

2. **Sit-ups (trunk endurance)**
   a) Lying on your back with your knees bent and hands clasped behind your head, sit up and touch your elbows to your knees.
   b) Your partner sits on your feet facing you with his hands clasped under your knees.
   c) Record the number of completed sit-ups in one minute.
   d) Good score: 55 repetitions.

3. Step ups (leg endurance)

a) Standing facing a 6″ stool, step up with your right foot, followed by your left foot, then down with your right foot, left foot.

b) Your partner counts the number of times both feet are together on the ground.

c) Record the number of completed step ups in one minute.

d) Good score: 40 repetitions.

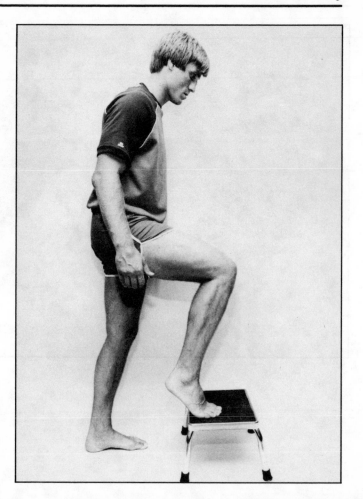

MUSCULAR STRENGTH:

1. **Maximum bench press**

   a) Lying with your back and buttocks flat on a bench, slowly lower the weight bar down across your chest and push up to extended arm position.

   b) Your partner acts as your "spotter."

   c) Record the maximum weight that you can successfully bench press once.

   d) Good score: Your weight plus 50 pounds.

2. Maximum leg extension

a) Sitting on a leg extension machine, slowly raise your legs to full extended knee position.

b) Record the maximum weight that you can successfully leg extend once.

c) Good score: Your weight plus 50 pounds.

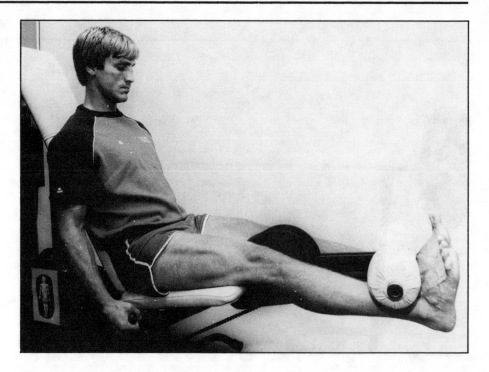

FLEXIBILITY:

1. **Hamstrings**
   a) Sitting with your legs straight and together, slowly bend forward and reach your fingertips toward your toes as far as possible.
   b) Your partner measures with a ruler the distance between your finger tips and your toes.
   c) Record the number of inches.
      - 0 inches when finger tips just reach toes.
      - Negative inches when fingertips don't reach toes.
      - Positive inches when fingertips reach past toes.
   d) Good score: Positive 5 inches.

2. Groin

   a) Sitting with your legs straight, slowly spread your legs apart as far as possible.

   b) Your partner measures with a tape measure the distance between your knees.

   c) Record the number of inches.

   d) Good score: 30 inches.

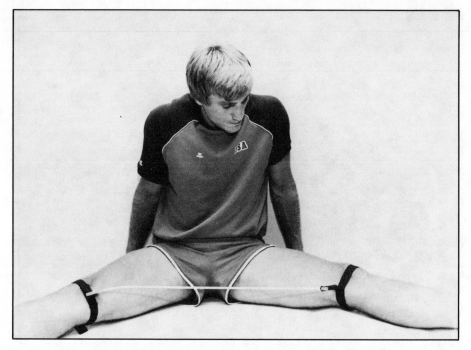

POWER:

1. Vertical jump

a) Measure and mark on board mounted on a wall from 0 inches at ground level to 120 inches (10 feet high).

b) Standing next to the "reach board" with both heels on floor, reach as high as possible. Your partner records this starting height.

c) Now from a crouched position, jump up as high as possible, touching the reach board. Your partner records the jumping height.

d) Record the distance in inches between the starting and jumping heights. Best of three attempts.

e) Good score: 20 inches.

GOALTENDERS ARE PLAYERS, TOO! 9

A common misconception of both players and spectators alike is that goaltenders need not be as physically fit as forwards and defensemen because they do not have to skate up and down the ice during the game. Nothing could be further from the truth! Not only must the goalie be as well conditioned as his teammates, but in some areas he must be in *better* condition than any other player on the ice.

While it is true that goalkeepers are not required to skate the great distances that skaters do, remember that those players are on the ice for no more than a minute or two at a time. The goalie, however, never gets a rest. He plays sixty minutes of stop time which means that he will spend up to two hours on the ice in an average game.

When you reach the play-offs, you have the added burden of overtime, and that's when a goalkeeper's conditioning is especially important. If you want an example of how tough it can be, just look at the 1982 Calder Cup playoffs in the American Hockey League. In consecutive play-off games between the Rochester Americans and New Haven Nighthawks, the two clubs played a double-overtime game in Rochester and a *quadruple*-over-time game in New Haven in a period of just over 48 hours. Can you imagine what it would be like if you were not in top condition and had to step on the ice for your *seventh* period of the game—at two o'clock in the morning?

In addition to never getting off the ice, the goalie must also carry about forty extra pounds of bulky equipment which only gets heavier as the game progresses—and it gets wet. He also must wield a stick that weighs three times as much as any other—and do so with just one hand instead of two. When the puck is in his end of the ice, the goalie spends most of his time stooped in an unnatural and physically stressful crouch while having to concentrate on the puck which may, at any instant come flying in his direction at a hundred miles an hour through a gaggle of pushing and shoving players. And he has to stop it before it enters the net.

If *that* doesn't require superb conditioning, nothing does! A goalkeeper who can't endure the physical and mental stresses and pressures of his position won't be a goaltender for long.

If you are a goaltender, you should follow exactly the same conditioning program as your teammates but with extra attention on developing strength—and especially *endurance*—in the calf, thigh, groin, lower back, forearm and wrist muscles. You should do extra flexibility training for the groin, lower back and arms.

The calves are the most important muscles for the goalie to develop. More than any other player, a goaltender depends on balance to be effective. But if he lacks endurance in the calves and they become fatigued, the goalie will soon find himself sitting back on his heels and most of that precious balance will be lost. Strong thighs are important to move your pad-shrouded legs quickly and accurately from side to side or when making kick saves.

Extra work on developing the forearms and wrists is needed because of the extra weight and bulk of the catching glove, blocker and goalkeeper's stick. No player on the ice is called upon to move his arms and hands faster—or more accurately—than the goalie. And he can't cheat—a missed puck is a goal.

Extreme flexibility in the groin and lower back is vital to a goalkeeper's success in that it enables him to cover more of the net and stop the puck more often. But perhaps even more importantly, it is a major factor in preventing groin pulls and muscle tears. No injury is more debilitating to a goalie than a groin or lower back injury—nor is any more easily prevented or reduced in severity by being maximally flexible.

Finally the goalkeeper should put particular emphasis on the development of overall physical endurance. No player on the ice is required to concentrate harder on what is going on around him than the goalie—and with far less margin for error. Mental alertness is often the first victim of fatigue and that is especially true between the pipes. The mind only has to wander for just an instant to make the difference between a save and a goal.

Close games are often decided in one or two brief flurries around the net. That's when the goalie's conditioning can make as much difference in stopping the puck as his skills. Far from being the least well-conditioned player on the ice, in many ways the goalie must be the best. He—and his teammates—cannot afford anything less.

CALF ENDURANCE:
1. HEEL RAISES
With the bar resting on your shoulder behind your neck, rise up onto your tiptoes, then slowly lower your heels to the ground. Your feet should be shoulder-width apart and the balls of your feet resting on a 2″ high board. Perform this exercise for 30 repetitions.

THIGH ENDURANCE:
1. LEG EXTENSIONS

Using some form of leg extension machine, slowly kick your legs up to the straight leg position. Perform this exercise for 30 repetitions.

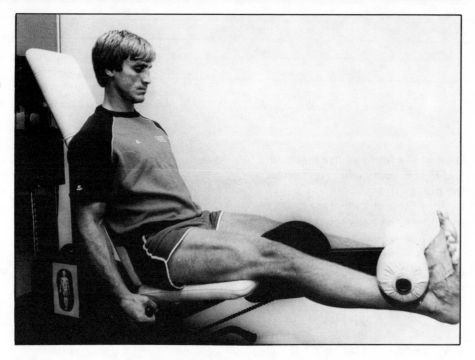

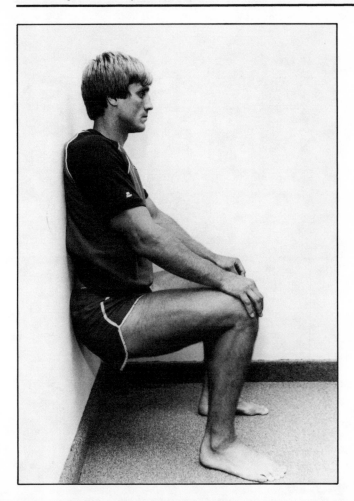

2. WALL SEAT
Leaning your back against a wall, assume a sitting position with your hips and knees both at right angles. Maintain this position for five minutes without moving.

FOREARM AND WRIST ENDURANCE:

1. WRIST ROLLS

With a five or ten pound weight hanging from a bar, roll the weight up the bar, then unwind the weight by slowly rolling your wrists in the opposite direction. Perform this exercise for ten repetitions with your palms up and then ten repetitions with your palms facing down.

2. FIGURE 8'S

With a two or five pound weight attached to the end of a broken hockey stick, grasp the handle of the stick and draw a three foot high figure 8 in the air using only your wrists, not your shoulders. Perform 10 repetitions in both directions.

As we noted earlier, winning isn't everything but the *effort* to win is. If you are not willing to put honest—and consistent—effort into your conditioning program, the desired results will not be there. Even a little bit of cheating makes a big difference in the end results because most of the benefits of this program are derived *only* when each exercise is done to the extreme limit of your ability to do it. Virtually *all* improvement in each area will be the result of pushing beyond the maximum you reached in your previous workout.

The best way to prevent yourself from cheating is to keep a thorough record of each day in a diary. We have prepared such a diary in the form of three simple charts which cover off-season, pre-season, and in-season programs. The diary in the back of this book will take you through 3 one-month periods of conditioning. (Additional sets can be made by photocopy.)

You will note that every training routine is preceded and followed by a box marked flexibility. Enter there which of the four flexibility regimens (solo, partner, locker, or wet) was completed.

OFF-SEASON DIARY:

Each off-season diary sheet covers a period of four weeks and is divided into two sections for each week's workouts. The upper two-thirds covers thrice weekly strength training (Monday, Wednesday, and Friday) while the lower third is for recording twice weekly aerobic (endurance) training (Tuesday and Thursday). You will note that this leaves weekends free to do as you please, but we recommend you spend some of that time engaged in recreational athletic activity such as handball, racquetball, tennis, soccer, or basketball. Activities such as these not only help maintain conditioning but also help develop quickness, body control, acceleration and deceleration and other similar skills which are useful to hockey players.

Record the date and two (before and after) flexibility routines you plan to do as you start each day's workout. On days when you do strength training, enter the eleven exercises you have selected. Record the weight (in pounds) and number of repetitions of the *third* set (at 100 percent level) of each exercise in the diary.

On days when you do aerobic (endurance) training, enter the number of minutes (minimum: 15) worked and the distance you covered in miles (running) or laps (swimming).

PRE-SEASON DIARY:

As with the off-season diary, each sheet of the pre-season diary covers a period of four weeks and is divided into two sections. The upper section now covers muscular endurance conditioning done three times-a-week (Monday, Wednesday and Friday) in the form of circuit training. The lower section covers aerobic conditioning which is also done three times-a-week (Tuesday, Thursday, and Saturday) in the form of interval training.

On days when you do circuit training, list the exercises selected and note the maximum weight and, number of repetitions for each one. When doing interval training, simply record the time spent and the total number of intervals completed.

IN-SEASON DIARY:

Because of the irregularities involved in training during the playing season, the in-season diary is not divided into weeks. On training days fill in the date and the weight/ repetition OR minutes/intervals depending on which training routine (circuit or interval) is followed.

We cannot overemphasize the importance of keeping a complete—and honest—diary of your training and conditioning program. It will not only tell you how well you are doing but should also help provide you with an incentive to keep on the right track.

OFF-SEASON DIARY

DATE	M.		W.		F.		M.		W.		F.		M.		W.		F.		M.		W.		F.	
FLEXIBILITY																								
STRENGTH TRAINING	wt.	reps	wt.	reps	wt.	reps	wt.	reps	wt.	reps	wt.	reps	wt.	reps	wt.	reps	wt.	reps	wt.	reps	wt.	reps	wt.	reps
1.																								
2.																								
3.																								
4.																								
5.																								
6.																								
7.																								
8.																								
9.																								
10.																								
11.																								
FLEXIBILITY																								

DATE	T.		TH.		T.		TH.		T.		TH.		T.		TH.	
FLEXIBILITY																
AREOBIC TRAINING	mins	dist	mins	dist	mins	dist	mins	dist	mins	dist	mins	dist	mins	dist	mins	dist
FLEXIBILITY																

PRE-SEASON DIARY

DATE	M.		W.		F.		M.		W.		F.		M.		W.		F.		M.		W.		F.	
FLEXIBILITY																								
CIRCUIT TRAINING	wt.	reps	wt.	reps	wt.	reps	wt.	reps	wt.	reps	wt.	reps	wt.	reps	wt.	reps	wt.	reps	wt.	reps	wt.	reps	wt.	reps
1.																								
2.																								
3.																								
4.																								
5.																								
6.																								
7.																								
8.																								
9.																								
10.																								
11.																								
FLEXIBILITY																								

DATE	T.		Th.		S.		T.		Th.		S.		T.		Th.		S.		T.		Th.		S.	
FLEXIBILITY																								
INTERVAL TRAINING	mins	int	mins	int	mins	int	mins	int	mins	int	mins	int	mins	int	mins	int	mins	int	mins	int	mins	int	mins	int
FLEXIBILITY																								

IN-SEASON DIARY

DATE	M.		W.		F.		M.		W.		F.		M.		W.		F.		M.		W.		F.	
FLEXIBILITY																								
CIRCUIT TRAINING	wt.	reps	wt.	reps	wt.	reps	wt.	reps	wt.	reps	wt.	reps	wt.	reps	wt.	reps	wt.	reps	wt.	reps	wt.	reps	wt.	reps
1.																								
2.																								
3.																								
4.																								
5.																								
6.																								
7.																								
8.																								
9.																								
10.																								
11.																								
INTERVAL TRAINING	mins	int	mins	int	mins	int	mins	int	mins	int	mins	int	mins	int	mins	int	mins	int	mins	int	mins	int	mins	int
FLEXIBILITY																								

GLOSSARY

Aerobic exercise—exercise during which the energy required is supplied by the oxygen inspired (sustained period of vigorous activity).

Anaerobic exercise—exercise during which the energy required is provided without the utilization of inspired oxygen (short bursts of vigorous activity).

Cardiovascular endurance—the ability of the heart and lungs to supply oxygen to the working muscles for a sustained period of time.

Cardiovascular sytem—the heart, lungs, and circulatory system.

Circuit training—a series of high intensity exercise drills performed sequentially with minimal rest between exercise stations.

Fartlek training—varying the speed, resistance, tempo of continuous training while maintaining the heart rate in the target zone.

Flexibility—the ability to bend and stretch without breaking.

In-season—period beginning the first day of training camp and ending with the last game.

Intensity—the degree of effort.

Interval training—alternating high intensity activity with relief periods while maintaining the heart rate in the target zone.

Maximum heart rate—220 minus age.

Muscular endurance—the ability to exert force for a sustained period of time.

Muscular strength—the ability to exert force.

Off-season—period beginning the day after the last game and ending six weeks prior to training camp.

Overload principle—progressively increasing the training resistance (weights) to stimulate greater strength.

Power—the ability to exert force quickly.

Pre-season—period beginning six weeks prior to training camp and ending the first day of training camp.

Reciprocal inhibition—maximally contracting a muscle to facilitate relaxation of the opposite muscle to be stretched.

Repetitions—the number of times an exercise is performed.

Sprain—an overstretching or tearing of a ligament.

Strain—an overstretching or tearing of a muscle.

Target zone—between 70 percent to 85 percent of maximum heart rate.

Ten RM—10 Repetition Maximum—the maximum weight one can lift 10 times.

ABOUT THE AUTHORS

PAT CROCE

Pat Croce, the NHL's first physical conditioning coach, is one of America' leading young physical fitness professionals. In 1981, at the age of 26, he was appointed Physical Conditioning Coach for the Philadelphia Flyers of the National Hockey League. He is responsible for the physical conditioning and rehabilitation programs of both the Flyers and their American Hockey League development club, the Maine Mariners. Croce also serves as Administrative Director of the Sports Medicine Clinic at Haverford Community Hospital in nearby Havertown, PA, and is President of Tone Up, Inc., The Fitness Consultants.

A native of Philadelphia, Pat Croce is a cum laude graduate of the University of Pittsburgh (B.S.). A licensed Physical Therapist (LPT) and Certified Athletic Trainer (ATC), he is also an elected member of both the American College of Sports Medicine and the National Strength and Conditioning Association. As an active competitive athlete he was two-time United States National Light-weight Karate Champion.

His previous publications include a monograph entitled *Stretch Your Life.*

ABOUT THE AUTHORS

BRUCE C. COOPER

An experienced hockey writer and administrator, Bruce Cooper has written about hockey and other sports for numerous newspapers and magazines. A Philadelphia native, he is a graduate of Temple University (B.Sc., 1968) where he also did graduate work in communications. He taught English and writing at the William Penn Charter School in Philadelphia and was later an administrator at Haverford College in nearby Haverford, PA., before devoting full time to writing and sports administration.

He was formerly Director of Press and Public Relations for the Philadelphia Firebirds and from 1979 to 1982 wrote a column

entitled SCOOP for the Philadelphia Flyers' program magazine, *Goal*. His previous publications also include the Flyers' 1979-1980, 1980-81 and 1981-82 Yearbooks.

His activities as a free lance writer take him to as many as 125 major and minor league professional, college and amateur hockey games a season. He is also President of both Cooper-Clement Associates, Ardmore, PA, and Radiological Imaging Corporation, Los Angeles, CA.